D1733361

ANIMALS OF THE DESERT

Sand Cats

by Patrick Perish

BELLWETHER MEDIA • MINNEAPOLIS, MN

Blastoff! Readers are carefully developed by literacy experts to build reading stamina and move students toward fluency by combining standards-based content with developmentally appropriate text.

Level 1 provides the most support through repetition of high-frequency words, light text, predictable sentence patterns, and strong visual support.

Level 2 offers early readers a bit more challenge through varied sentences, increased text load, and text-supportive special features.

Level 3 advances early-fluent readers toward fluency through increased text load, less reliance on photos, advancing concepts, longer sentences, and more complex special features.

★ **Blastoff! Universe**

Reading Level

Grade **K**

Grades **1–3**

Grade **4**

This edition first published in 2021 by Bellwether Media, Inc.

No part of this publication may be reproduced in whole or in part without written permission of the publisher. For information regarding permission, write to Bellwether Media, Inc., Attention: Permissions Department, 6012 Blue Circle Drive, Minnetonka, MN 55343.

Library of Congress Cataloging-in-Publication Data

Names: Perish, Patrick, author.
Title: Sand cats / by Patrick Perish.
Description: Minneapolis, MN : Bellwether Media, Inc., 2021. | Series: Blastoff! readers: animals of the desert | Includes bibliographical references and index. | Audience: Ages 5-8 | Audience: Grades K-1 | Summary: "Relevant images match informative text in this introduction to sand cats. Intended for students in kindergarten through third grade"-- Provided by publisher.
Identifiers: LCCN 2019054249 (print) | LCCN 2019054250 (ebook) | ISBN 9781644872215 (library binding) | ISBN 9781618919793 (ebook)
Subjects: LCSH: Cats--Arid regions--Juvenile literature.
Classification: LCC QL737.C23 P3777 2021 (print) | LCC QL737.C23 (ebook) | DDC 599.75--dc23
LC record available at https://lccn.loc.gov/2019054249
LC ebook record available at https://lccn.loc.gov/2019054250

Text copyright © 2021 by Bellwether Media, Inc. BLASTOFF! READERS and associated logos are trademarks and/or registered trademarks of Bellwether Media, Inc.

Editor: Rebecca Sabelko   Designer: Josh Brink

Printed in the United States of America, North Mankato, MN.

Table of Contents

Life in the Desert

Sand cats are **mammals** that live in deserts from northern Africa to central Asia.

These small cats hunt in this dry **biome**.

Sand Cat Range

range =

N
W E
S

Deserts are hot during
the day and cold at night.
Thick fur helps sand cats stay
the right **temperature**.

Their light-colored fur also acts as **camouflage**. It helps keep the cats safe from **predators**.

Sand cats have thick fur on the bottoms of their feet. The fur keeps them from getting burned by hot ground.

It also keeps the cats from sinking into the desert sands.

Special Adaptations

large ears

thick, light-colored fur

furry feet

Sand Cats at Home

Sand cats are **nocturnal**. They hunt at night when the desert is cooler.

They rest in **burrows**
to stay cool during the day.

burrow

Before sand cats leave
their burrows, they
watch for predators.

The cats do not leave
until it is safe.

Desert Hunters

Sand cats eat **rodents**, birds, and **insects**.

The cats use their wide ears to hear rodents below the ground. They dig fast to catch their dinner.

Sand Cat Diet

desert locusts

desert larks

lesser Egyptian jerboas

These cats quietly watch for **prey** before they **pounce**.

They bury extra food
to eat later.

There is little water in the desert. Sand cats can go a long time without drinking.

They get most of the water they need from their prey.

Sand Cat Stats

Least Concern	Near Threatened	Vulnerable	Endangered	Critically Endangered	Extinct in the Wild	Extinct

conservation status: least concern

life span: 4 years

Sand cats will even take on **venomous** snakes! The cats quickly strike at the snakes' heads.

These fierce cats are **adapted** to desert life!

Glossary

adapted—well suited due to changes over a long period of time

biome—a large area with certain plants, animals, and weather

burrows—holes or tunnels some animals dig for homes

camouflage—coloring or markings that make animals look like their surroundings

insects—small animals with six legs and hard outer bodies; an insect's body is divided into three parts.

mammals—warm-blooded animals that have backbones and feed their young milk

nocturnal—active at night

pounce—to suddenly jump on something to catch it

predators—animals that hunt other animals for food

prey—animals that are hunted by other animals for food

rodents—small animals that gnaw on their food

temperature—a measurement of hot and cold

venomous—able to poison its prey

To Learn More

AT THE LIBRARY

Perish, Patrick. *Fennec Foxes*. Minneapolis, Minn.: Bellwether Media, 2019.

Topacio, Francine. *Creatures in a Hot Desert*. New York, N.Y.: PowerKids Press, 2020.

Wilkins, Mary-Jane. *Deserts*. Tucson, Ariz.: Brown Bear Books, 2017.

ON THE WEB

FACTSURFER

Factsurfer.com gives you a safe, fun way to find more information.

1. Go to www.factsurfer.com.

2. Enter "sand cats" into the search box and click 🔍.

3. Select your book cover to see a list of related content.

Index

The images in this book are reproduced through the courtesy of: Vladislav T. Jirousek, front cover (hero); geogif, front cover (background), pp. 2-3; Gerard Lacz Images/ SuperStock, pp. 4, 19; Arco Images GmbH/ Alamy, p. 6; Thomas Rabeil/ Minden, p. 7; Nature Picture Library/ Alamy, p. 8; Edo Schmidt/ Alamy, p. 9; Malcolm Schuyl/ Alamy, p. 10; Elena Moiseeva, p. 11; cgwp.co.uk/ Alamy, pp. 12, 18; Edwin Giesbers/ Alamy, p. 13; Alain Dragesco-Joffe/ Nature Picture Library, pp. 14, 20; Guillermo Guerao Serra, p. 15 (top left); Gergo Nagy, p. 15 (top right); Konrad Wothe/ Alamy, p. 15 (bottom); Gerard Lacz/Mauritius/ SuperStock, p. 16; Mike Lane/ Alamy, p. 17; Arco/G.Lacz/ Alamy, p. 21; Photononstop/ SuperStock, p. 23.